A Century in Steam

Bryan Holden and Kenneth H. Leech

No.6012 *King Edward VI* with the Plymouth to Paddington non-stop express, between Savernake and Wolf Hall, on 26 July 1961. The Kennet and Avon canal on the right ran under the trackbed and emerged on the north side of the line.

IRWELL
PRESS

Dedication

FOR GLADYS & BARBARA

without whose understanding and forbearance these ventures would not have been possible.

'YOU'LL NEVER DIE: THEY'LL HAVE TO SHOOT YOU!'

(Driver Bill Bateman speaking to 68 year-old Kenneth Leech after he had fired non-stop from Paddington to Reading in 41 minutes for the 36 miles, with a signal check at Reading East, costing 3 minutes. The locomotive was No.5068 Beverston Castle hauling a 15 coach train, 505 tons tare load, 50 tons over the limit for a Castle).

Published by
IRWELL PRESS
3 Durley Avenue, Pinner, Middlesex, HA5 1JQ
Printed by Amadeus Press Ltd., Huddersfield

CONTENTS

Kenneth Leech, aged 2. Photographed on his second birthday in 1894, the infant Kenneth, would not have his picture taken without his toy engine. 'Since then, over my whole life, I have *Never* been without a model loco. My lifelong enthusiasm for steam engines was kindled almost before I could walk.'

Introduction

After publication of our third book of Great Western locomotives, 'Portraits of Western 4-6-0s', back in 1983, Kenneth and I felt we had brought down the final curtain on our joint authorship. For some seven years we had shared our rail experiences, albeit gained in such widely differing circumstances: Kenneth in a unique and highly privileged position as unofficial driver and fireman on many and varied top-link express locomotives in the West Country; myself as

a keen trackside observer, mainly on the Paddington-Birmingham (Snow Hill) line, which in the 'forties and 'fifties was a major rail artery between the two cities.

Despite numerous appeals from our readers, we felt unable to commit ourselves to further literary endeavour. The increasing demands of an expanding business on my part, along with Kenneth's feelings that at 91 years of age he had said all there was to be said about his footplate experiences de-

cided we should call it a day, proud to rest on our laurels in the hope we had made some small contribution to an already vast archive of railway lore.

From this it must not be construed (for it would be entirely untrue) that we had in any way grown tired of our mutual collaboration. Far from it; we had both enjoyed ourselves immensely over so many years, and had savoured the compilation of the books as one might a vintage wine. Or, to employ a sporting metaphor, like batsmen at the crease we had concentrated on building a solid partnership. There had been occasional flurries of activity when we had taken the word count along at a steady pace, followed by quieter periods (usually because of my business commitments) and then, suddenly, we'd spring into action with a series of well-struck boundaries. And we'd feel exhilarated at seeing the scoreboard of the manuscript grow page by page.

For new readers, the manner in which Kenneth and I first came together might be of some interest; but it is not my wont to repeat verbatim the account of our meeting, for it has already been set down in some detail in a previous work. Suffice to say, it was an interest in No.7029 *Clun Castle* that effected our introduction, in the middle 1970s. At that time I was seeking photographs of No.7029, as she was in her BR working days and I came to know of Kenneth Leech as someone who had taken many thousands of photographs of Great Western engines, and, therefore, quite likely to have one or two of *Clun Castle*.

From his huge collection of negatives it was not surprising that Kenneth was able to meet my needs. On meeting for the first time, we struck up an immediate rapport and the seeds of our initial collaboration, 'Portraits of Kings', were well and truly sown.

The 'Kings' was not an easy book to write, or, for that matter, an easy concept to sell to a publisher. It featured all thirty engines of the 6000 class, at first glance looking all the same, but individually the photographs showed each locomotive as built with single chimney, and later, following improved draughting modifications, as fitted with double-chimney, a unique record of the GWR's flagship class of express locomotive.

We were helped in our task by Richard (Dick) Potts, a former Tyseley (GWR) engineman who had made his job his hobby,

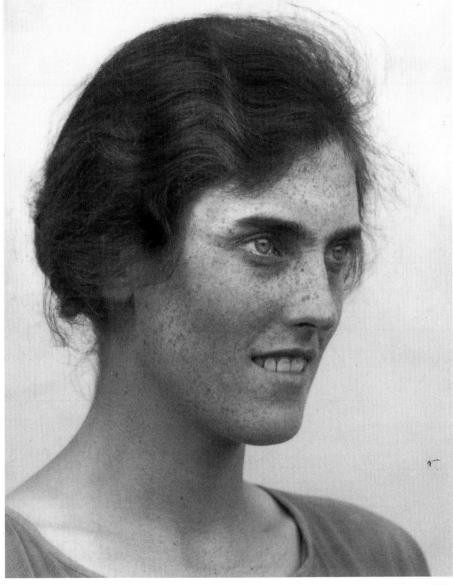

Kenneth's wife Gladys: 'She has been even more — *much* more tied-up with my life than steam locos. I owe her so much for her constant love and understanding'.

No.4975 *Umberslade Hall* A superb picture as No.4975 struggles up Whiteball with the 11.10 am *Cornishman* with 14 coaches from Penzance to Wolverhampton on 7 August 1954. Quite a feat to go over the top blowing-off and no blower on! It must have been a cold day to show steam so well.

No.5081 *Lockheed Hudson*. The *Bristolian* with an empty train draws into Temple Meads Station, Bristol from the carriage sidings. The point of interest is headboard with the crown and 'ER' motif. This was carried only during 1953 to commemorate the Coronation of Her Majesty Queen Elizabeth II.

insomuch as he had kept a detailed journal of every steam locomotive he worked on. Dick Potts has an eagle-eye and an encyclopaedic memory for the finer points of mechanical detail, gained first-hand working on the footplate, both as fireman and driver.

Eventually we produced a manuscript which not only catalogued the technicalities of the 'Kings', and might therefore be of assistance to model-makers and railway artists, but also a warm-hearted personalised account of some of the many enginemen who had handled these magnificent machines in everyday service, and with whom Kenneth, following his retirement as Chief Mechanical Engineer of the Westinghouse Brake and Signal Company, had developed a close friendship and travelled an incredible 45,000 route miles, often sharing the footplate duties.

From the outset, I felt it was important to get a first-hand account of Kenneth's long association with enginemen and their locomotives, and the best way of doing this, I believed, was simply to sit and talk with him, taping the conversation on an unobtrusively-placed cassette recorder.

Kenneth was the perfect interviewee, always totally relaxed and utterly decisive in everything he said, his recall of past events crystal clear, as he poured forth a stream of experiences and anecdotes without hesitation, at dictation speed. Obviously, he was reliving every moment, and, at times, became quite animate, rising from his armchair and miming the shovelling of coal from an imaginary tender and shooting it with practised ease the length of a firebox.

Always I was welcomed most warmly by Kenneth's charming wife, who realising my need for refreshment after the long car journey from the Midlands, would tap on the door of the 'railway room' with a tray of tea, enquiring whether I took sugar, and did I like Earl Grey, or would I prefer a milder blend? Even before I'd taken the first sip, Kenneth would pick-up the narrative at the point of interruption and he'd be off again in

This was the first of many thousands of photographs which Kenneth Leech took of GWR locomotives. In May 1946 this veteran 2-4-0 tank engine appeared on the Chippenham to Calne job. She caught Kenneth's special interest as being a unique survivor of the engines of his boyhood days, back in the 1890s. Shed code BL (Bath Road, Bristol) is just visible on the frame though No 1499 had recently been transferred to Swindon. She was withdrawn and scrapped about a month after this photograph was taken.

No.4053 *Princess Alexandra* at Thingley in June 1952. No.4053 is being run-in on the 5.00pm Swindon to Bristol after general repairs. The engine remained in service for another two years.

Stan Morris was Works Engineman Foreman at Swindon. He was responsible for preparing locomotives in readiness for entering the repair shop. 'Stan made possible all my Swindon photographs of locos in mint condition' says Kenneth. 'Most Sundays he would place three repaired and newly painted engines in suitable positions for me to photograph.'

full flow.

There were moments of light relief, too, when Kenneth would break-off from recording to play one of his many musical compositions on the pianola. I will ever cherish memories of seeing him seated upright at the piano keyboard, his feet paddling the pedals, the piano keys rising and falling, as though played by ghostly hands. Kenneth's repertoire runs to a great variety of chamber music, music for full orchestra (he has conducted several of the latter in public concerts) and over 160 solo songs. Many of these he has painstakingly transcribed onto rolls of greaseproof paper using a specially constructed small T-square, with a notch for each note, and a razor blade, each piece of music taking several days to cut.

Sometimes I was accompanied by Dick Potts, and then Kenneth would be at his most ebullient; for Dick is also a lover of classical music. It was times like these, when Kenneth and Dick were totally en-grossed with music and railways, that I enjoyed the most. For then I could let the recorder run full measure, with just an occasional interjection should I wish to clarify a particular point, or pursue a line of interesting discussion.

I found it fascinating to observe the physical change in Kenneth as he went back in time, describing incidents that had happened sixty, seventy years before, and recounting them with such certainty of recollection, as though they had taken place only yesterday. His voice and demeanour would take on a more authoritative tone as he recalled some of his many official and unofficial dealings with the key personalities in the world of locomotive engineering – Cook, Smeddle and Hawksworth of the Great Western; Bullied in the First World War, in France, and on the Southern Railway, and the leonine, silver-haired doyen of the LNER, and precursor of the streamlined locomotive, Sir Nigel Gresley, during the General Strike in 1928.

Kenneth recalled one particular meeting at King's Cross with Bert Spencer, a long-standing friend of his and Gresley's personal assistant. The telephone rang and Spencer was called into the great man's office, and returned a few minutes later smiling broadly. There had been an urgent report on an unstreamlined 'Pacific' engine that had just made a record run. Sir Nigel was delighted. 'There, I knew it!' he had exclaimed. 'I don't need to cover my locomotives in bits of tin to make them go faster – but it makes them look so much better in the public's eye!'

Following the publication of 'Portraits of Kings', the demand from enthusiasts for copies of Kenneth's locomotive photographs grew apace, and I became concerned at the trust he placed in so many unknown individuals to whom he loaned his precious negatives. But such is the nature of the man no-one took advantage of him, rather he made many new friends. 'I belong to a bygone era', he would say. 'And I'm only too

No.6020 *King Henry IV* entering Box Tunnel (West end) on 25 June 1961. 'Driver Griffin (Swindon) was in charge, but I was doing the firing.'

No.5050 *Earl of St Germans*. An up express entering Temple Meads, Bristol. The LMS Class 5 locomotive on the left had just arrived from the north and uncoupled from its train. 'I once asked a driver on No.5050 what sort of an engine she was, and after a moment's thought he replied: 'Just like her number, fifty-fifty!'

No.4056 *Princess Margaret* An historic moment. No. 4056 draws into Temple Meads, Bristol on 26 November 1955 after having made the fastest time recorded from Exeter to the top of Whiteball. 'O.S.Nock was on the footplate at the time, and told me this.'

pleased to share the treasury of my experiences, and see the fruits of my labours bringing pleasure and enlightenment to those of a new generation.'

But it is his tremendous zest for life that has impressed me most of all, his boundless enthusiasm for the task in hand, his incredible memory and his strength of purpose. I asked him the secret of his longevity. 'Keep the muscle of your brain alive and active', he answered, lightly.

Designing the format of the books and putting Kenneth's words onto paper has been solely my responsibility, along with the research into the history of each locomotive. From the outset Kenneth and I have insisted that we be involved in the presentation of the finished works, and fortunately our publishers have readily agreed − even taking on board our suggestions for photographic format and dust-jacket design.

Our second book, 'Portraits of Castles', like its predecessor, was the record of a whole class of Great Western express locomotive. It was distinguished in that Kenneth had photographed each and every one of the 171 Castles. Unfortunately, after Kings and Castles, Kenneth did not have enough photographs to complete other

classes of locomotive; and so, in our third collaboration, 'Portraits of Western 4-6-0s', we presented a representative selection which included Kings and Castles − and everything else. Whilst this might be seen as a pot-pourri, it was by no means a random selection; and it also enabled Kenneth to comment on his footplate experiences on every class of the Great Western's express locomotive stud.

Our latest book is different in so many ways from those which have gone before. For not only is it a tribute to the great days of steam in the West Country, it is also a singular evocation of a man's enjoyment of life after his working days are done. It is the heart-warming story of a man who has put the responsibilities and strictures of a top executive job behind him forever, and lived to the full a schoolboy's dream of riding on the footplate of the giants of steam.

Here we find Kenneth at the lineside photographing such famous trains as The Bristolian, the Cornish Riviera and the Royal Duchy, always with his enginemen friends acknowledging his presence. We find him at his favourite lineside locations: Box, Savernake, Cole, Thingley Junction and Whiteball Summit. There is much evi-

dence of his beloved Chippenham; Regency Bath; Brunel's great architectural edifice, Temple Meads, Bristol, and, of course, Swindon, the cathedral of Great Western steam.

This personal choice of photographs has captured rare moments of locomotives on test; shots of 'foreign' engines on the Western Region; and an abundance of all sorts of locomotive performances in all sorts of conditions.

But perhaps the most important aspect of this book is the story of the enginemen − a special breed of British workman which has passed into history with the demise of the Steam Age.

This is Kenneth Leech's personal documentary. Never again shall we see the likes of such engines. Never again will there be another like, or so lucky, as Kenneth Leech.

It is a privilege to know him so well and to have shared the pleasure and enjoyment in setting down this unique record.

Bryan Holden
Solihull
July 1992

Mixed traffic 2-8-0 No.4708 viewed from the road overbridge at Whiteball.

No.6015 *King Richard III* just east of Chippenham Station with the 11.15 am down *Merchant Venturer* on 1 September 1954. Speed about 75 mph.

No.5091 *Cleeve Abbey*. A stirring sight, as No.5091 storms out of Box Tunnel with the 9.15 am ex-Paddington express on 18 October 1952. Speed was recorded at 71 mph.

Lineside Locations

It would be a mistake to think that Kenneth Leech spent all his available time riding hither and thither on the footplate, for it must be appreciated he was also an expert and committed photographer, and took thousands of photographs of trains and individual locomotives in all sorts of conditions and in a variety of locations, which he also processed and printed. It was photography that first introduced him to enginemen, when he took pictures of them on locomotives in Chippenham Station, particularly on the 5.00 pm running-in turn from Swindon. He would straightaway go home and process the films, so that in a couple of days he could present the crew with a set of prints, which, most likely, they would treasure for the rest of their lives.

To exhibit the engine to best advantage was always his aim, whether as a standing portrait or on a train at speed. Background pleasant, if convenient, foreground not obtrusive, and the crew, if willing, and providing it did not interfere with their duties.

Such was the simple philosophy which inspired Kenneth's long-running photographic mission.

But was he looking to achieve a particular photographic effect, or was the time and the moment the over-riding priority? Kenneth's answer is disarmingly simple: 'I never really concerned myself with photographic effects, only insofar as choosing the best available background. But the chosen spot, in practically all cases where a single shot of one especial train or engine was my aim, had to be handy to get at and within short distance of Chippenham.'

Whiteball, undoubtedly, was his favourite location. 'Plenty of trains, not going too fast; half a dozen viewpoints to vary the interest and, not least, a handy and convenient road or lane to park the car. And lots of fresh air! On a summer Saturday there was a train of interest every five minutes, up or down. Cole and Savernake were friendly spots, too, but had not the variety of viewpoint that Whiteball had.'

Such was Kenneth's enthusiasm that he photographed in all seasons and all weathers, except heavy rain. Not only could one not hope to get a good picture in rain, but Kenneth cherished his camera too much to risk damaging it through getting wet.

Asked to describe a typical Summer's day by the lineside he reminisced: 'So many summer outings were happy and similar that to describe a particular one is just not possible. But on a number of *long-distance* away trips one often met friends from the Midlands and even from London, for those special weekends just before August Bank Holiday. And the weather was always fine!

'Talk, food, camera ready, if not in hand, and a feeling of being safe to get home in a procession of 3 or 4 cars on the long return journey. On one or two trips, wives and small boys were also present.'

From this it will be seen that Kenneth enjoyed sharing his love of railways: he was by no means a lone wolf, and recalls only one occasion in the Chippenham area when

No.6028 *King George VI.* **'Stop!' 'Go!' No.6028 at Whiteball with the 12.05 pm Paddington to Plymouth express on 7 August 1954. Tank engine No.5157 waits to get into position for another banking duty.**

No.2920 *Saint David* nearing the end of her long career, and seen running into Chippenham on 14 September 1951 after her last general repair. Most of the Saints put up very high mileages, but with 2,080,754 miles 'on the clock' No. 2920 held the record.

No.7015 *Carn Brea Castle* leaving Box Tunnel with a down express.

No.7916 *Mobberley Hall* was the first Hall to be used in improved draughting trials, having jumper top wedged down at first. Here she heads the 8.06 am Sheffield to Kingswear at Whiteball on 23 March 1955.

No.6908 *Downham Hall* tackles the Whiteball incline with the 10.05 am Penzance to Liverpool on 7 August 1954.

No.6987 *Shervington Hall* It is interesting that the safety valve on No.6987 was just blowing off although the train had completed the ascent of the bank from Burlescombe to Whiteball. The engine was one of the first ten Halls to be fitted with improved draughting, as evidenced by the narrower chimney. She was pulling the 1.40 pm Paignton to Paddington on 23 July 1955.

No.7909 *Heveningham Hall* is seen in original condition with wider chimney, before re-draughting (See No. 6987 for comparison). She is working the 10.00 am Torquay to Birmingham on 6 August 1955. 'Just as a steam loco should be — working hard up a gradient, but no sign of a leak of steam anywhere.'

No.1025 *County of Radnor* with the 1.40 pm special from Kingswear to Paddington on Saturday, 11 August 1956. Here the train is at Brewham summit between Taunton and Westbury. By now, some Counties were in BR green-lined livery later extended to all members of the class. The coaches seem to be all new BR stock.

he was alone. 'Going further afield I always made sure I had a companion — for company and because I never have been able, cheerfully, to rely on a car not to give trouble, and someone to help diagnose and perhaps even repair the fault (if electrical!) was a comfort.'

Certainly this comment highlights the situation prevailing in the late 'fifties when new motor cars were in short supply, and to own a motor car was a money-draining luxury which demanded that one was able to service and maintain it in running order without the assistance of a garage mechanic.

In Winter most of Kenneth's visits to photograph trains at speed were local trips, often with a view to photographing a particular driver friend on the train. Usually there was the prospect of a footplate ride between Bath and Chippenham on the return working. He was prepared for a cold but short wait for his train, but only if the weather was practicable for photography. Certainly not in fog or a heavy snow-storm,

but on one or two occasions he was lucky and took some excellent pictures in flurries of snow.

Whilst it must have been exciting waiting for an express at the top of Whiteball Summit, surely after a while, there must have been a feeling of predictability about the likelihood of the locomotive being a particular Castle or King? 'To some extent, that is true,' said Kenneth, in reply. 'But I am ever the optimist in life, and on occasion something rather special would turn up unexpectedly, perhaps a Grange or even a 4700 on a really heavy long distance express train.'

But the sight and sound of an express working hard up the gradient never palled. However, one drawback of Whiteball, as a lineside location, as far as Kenneth was concerned, was the fact that he never saw a driver he knew, even on the *Riviera*. That was where Savernake scored for the down trains slowed by the immediately previous curve, and he could get good shots of the crew, Old Oak Common men, of course.

Rather like an artist or painter, Kenneth Leech developed a characteristic style in his locomotive photography. He liked best the normal view of an engine and train approaching, and abhorred views taken from low or very low levels, which although some might consider artistic did not show the engine or train satisfactorily, but portrayed a distorted and out of balance object.

What sort of shot gave him the most pleasure?
'I think, getting a last good view of a condemned Churchward Saint or Star working a train. Perhaps also a shot of a driver on his last pre-retirement trip.' Thankfully, for posterity, Kenneth seems always to have approached his work with a sense of history.

Savernake was a good second choice location, after Whiteball. It was a pleasant spot, Kenneth recalls, but there were fewer trains there than at Whiteball. However, it was convenient to leave the car at Wolf Hall and be able to patrol the whole length of lineside almost to Savernake Station. On one

No.6829 *Burmington Grange* heads the 12.18 pm Newton Abbot to Paddington at Whiteball on 7 August 1954.

No.5040 *Stokesay Castle* at Cole on 6 August 1955 with the 8.20 am Penzance to Paddington. She was being worked very hard, indeed. 'Three days later she worked the *Bristolian*, keeping time on the down trip at Dauntsey and gaining 4 minutes, in spite of four checks, on the up trip journey. The driver was my old friend Bill Brown.'

No.2945 *Hillingdon Court* 'This was the engine that first caught my attention and started my enthusiasm for taking photographs of Great Western engines.'

No.5055 *Earl of Eldon*. 'Certainly the worst smoke emission I ever saw on any GWR engine. I blame the fireman, even though the engine may have been in trouble and steaming poorly. I photographed No.5055 in this sorry state at Langley Crossing on 13 August 1949 on a Wolverhampton to Paddington express.'

occasion an up express was halted at Savernake advance starter and Kenneth knowing the driver well had quite a chat, even after the signal had been pulled off!

Kennet and Avon canal alongside the railway, the tunnelling under it, was picturesque, but there was no traffic on it, or on the former MSWJR line crossing the Great Western main line and running from Swindon to Andover.

Cole, with the Somerset and Dorset overbridge with only an occasional train, was also a pleasant place, but not an exciting spot for down trains. Up trains were on a curve so that photographs taken on the inside of the curve had to be taken against the light. Kenneth regards his luckiest shot at Cole was in having an S & D train crossing the bridge coinciding with the arrival of the down *Riviera*. This was an opportunist event: probably a unique shot.

Thingley Junction was only a minute or two from Chippenham, but car parking was difficult and Kenneth used it only as a vantage point for up trains of special interest, such as a condemned engine on the train and a few afternoon down trains. Only about two miles from Kenneth's house was Langley Crossing and signal box, but again used only for photographing trains, down and up, with a special engine or driver friend aboard.

Despite its Brunel facade and its excellence as a backdrop, Box Tunnel was not a regular location of Kenneth's. The few occasions on which he photographed a down train emerging from the tunnel were but to break a shopping trip to Bath! He would park his car a few yards away and go down the platelayers' path to the track to photograph a particular train due to pass, but he would never wait for another train.

And, once in a while, he would park the car a mile or so nearer Bath and photograph a side view of a down express on the long but low, embankment leading to Bathampton Station with a background of pleasant hills, dark enough to show off the steam.

Finally, Kenneth was invited, during one of the Bath Festivals, to photograph the special down train with its elaborate smokebox decoration from the signalbox high up above Bath Station down platform. And, of course, he also photographed the interior of the signalbox itself, this now only a memory of older travellers.

No.6002 *King William IV* heading the 8.15 am Perranporth to Paddington express at Cole on 11 August 1956. The engine is being worked extremely hard up the bank. The experimental sheet steel double chimney on No.6002 was replaced later by a cast iron version.

No.6001 *King Edward VII* races through Chippenham at around 75 mph on an improved-draughting test run with the 11.35 am
Paddington to Bristol express on 1 September 1953. Chief Inspector Pullen is waving from the cab as Kenneth takes the picture.
Note the dynamometer car behind the tender and the 'sleeve' in the chimney.

No.7029 *Clun Castle* on the 12.30 pm Paignton to Manchester express on 23 July 1955. The train is made up of an assortment of
LNER/GWR and LMS coaches.

No.6016 *King Edward V* passes the Box up distant signal at Shockerwick, sometime in 1955. Note sleeved chimney and forward position of mechanical lubricator.

No.6021 *King Richard II* almost at the top of the Whiteball climb with the Newquay to Paddington train on 7 August 1954. 'Safety valve is just sizzling, but in my view the fire needed more coal'.

No.4056 *Princess Margaret*, the last of the Stars, passing Hullavington on 11 February 1955. 'By then all the Saints and Stars, except this one had been withdrawn and cut-up. No.4056 was reduced to working gentle 'stopper' trains in her last days. She survived until October 1957.'

No.5063 *Earl Baldwin* and **No.4963** *Rignall Hall*. 'You go your way, and I'll go mine!' No.5063 with the 11.00 am Newquay to York express passing No.4963 at Whiteball sometime in 1955.'

2-8-0 No.4705 at Whiteball on 23 July 1955, heads the 7.pm Nottingham to Plymou train. Summer weekend often found the GWR hard-u for motive power and th 47XXs, not being required fo freight at the weekend, wer used on passenger trains.

'Once, on a passenger trai with a 47XX I was driving, hoped to reach 75 mph dow Dauntsey Bank, but th engine rode so appallingly was scared to exceed 65 mp Officially limited to 60 mp they rode very roughly abov that speed, due to the Cartaz axle boxes on the trailin coupled wheels.'

Churchward 2-6-2T No.4521 with a Taunton-Westbury local train at Creech, some-time in 1954.

53XX Class 'It was rare to se a 2-6-0 with express head lamps except perhaps on summer Saturday. I caugh this one at Whiteball Summi on 7 August 1954. It is prob able that the job was intende for a 4-6-0 which had either failed or was not ready i time. The fireman can be see on the right-hand side adjusting the injector. The locomotive was not going fa because there was too littl coal in the tender – maybe change at Bristol. The mix ture of LMS and GWR coaches suggests the train wa heading for the Midlands.'

Britannia Class 4-6-2 No.70015 *Apollo* at Whiteball on 7 August 1954 with the 11.00 am Paddington to Penzance express. Keen-eyed observers will notice that the sanders are still operating, though the train is well past the top of the bank. 'No comments permissible!'

2-8-0 No.4708 passing Cole on 6 August 1955 with the 1.20 pm Paddington to Kingswear. The engine is running easily down the gradient and is about to pass under the old Somerset and Dorset Railway overbridge.

2-8-0 No.4708 at Whiteball on 28 July 1956. The make-up of LMS coaches suggests the train was from the North or Midlands, but the locomotive would have come on the train at Bristol.

No.2912 *Saint Ambrose* is seen running into Chippenham with the train from Weymouth on 18 March 1950. This was a regular job for her, and Kenneth used to get up on the footplate in Chippenham Station before the engine drew the train into the siding east of the station. The locomotive was then turned on the turntable and placed clear for him to take photographs, before drawing the coaches into Chippenham down platform for the return trip to Weymouth.

No.2954 *Tockenham Court* looking rather down-at-heel on a parcels train, near Langley Crossing, in July 1952, the same month in which she was condemned. The engine was painted in BR black beneath the grime of neglect; but the enginemen had cleaned the name and numberplates in a forlorn attempt to give the old Saint a semblance of its former dignity!

No.4017 at Langley Crossing heading the 1.18 pm train from Paddington. She is in early BR condition with the engine number painted on the buffer beam. Her clean, shiny smokebox is typical of a recently ex-works engine. She was withdrawn and condemned in November 1949. 'This was my first attempt at photographing a GWR engine at speed.'

No.4038 *Queen Berengaria*. This was No.4038s last journey – from Westbury to Swindon and back – on 25 April 1952. 'I had ridden on her a fortnight earlier and found her very rough indeed at over 60 mph. The driver told me she had a cracked frame.'

No.1000 *County of Middlesex* on test with a 14 x 8 load (445 tons) running at 47 mph into a strong south-westerly wind. Steam made was 19,000 lbs per hour, at full regulator, 16 per cent cut-off.

As fitted with its original double chimney, No. 1000 was found unsatisfactory. The rest of the class were built with single chimneys and they steamed badly, too, and were given to losing time on passenger express trains, due to shortage of steam. 'Swindon seemed to have lost the knack of designing the steaming proportions needed, Manors, too, were originally poor steamers till taken in hand by the renowned S.O.Ell and his test department.'

2-8-0 No.3032 'A reminder of my old days in the Railway Operating Division (R.O.D.) Royal Engineers in the 1914-18 War, when among other duties my depot was working Dieppe docks. We received many of the engines from ships and ran them in on shunting duties until they were fit to work freight trains — ammunition and stores — inland via Serquex. None of those we had through our hands gave any trouble. I took this photograph at Thingley on 7 February 1953.'

No.4048 *Princess Victoria*. The lovely town of Bath in evening sunshine provides a pleasant background as No.4048 does a running-in turn from Swindon to Bristol and back. The picture as taken in 1952 and she was scrapped in January 1953.

No.1009 *County of Carmarthen* on an up train with a 16 x 8 test load at Hullavington in September 1954. The locomotive is fitted with a temporary double chimney.

'There is no doubt that this wretched type of double chimney ruined the appearance of the class, but I was told by the test department that they had expected the drawing office to raise the blast pipe and chimney to full loading gauge dimensions. However, it revolutionised and greatly improved the steaming of the class, which previously had been very poor.'

No.92178 a BR Standard 2-10-0, on a 14-coach controlled road test train at Hullavington on 30 January 1958. The brakes have been partially applied to increase tractive resistance. Note the dynamometer car behind tender, and also that no indicator diagrams are being taken.

2-8-0 No.3809 'The only photograph I ever took at Badminton Station. It was on 12 August 1956 and I had not expected a down train of empty stock hauled by a 2-8-0, but it was sometimes necessary during the summer shortage of locomotives.'

No.4056 *Princess Margaret* on the 4.15 pm down at Langley Crossing on 6 June 1952. 'It was unusual to see a Star on a regular Castle turn, but even more interesting is the mix of coaches – the first is an early LMS and the second a GWR 70ft Dreadnought.'

No.4055 *Princess Sophia* passing through Langley Crossing with the 1.18 pm ex-Paddington express sometime in 1947. The engine is still in Great Western livery, but the coaching stock is LMS. 'My second attempt at taking a GWR engine at speed! I estimated the train was travelling at about 60 mph and as an experiment I panned the camera to half that speed.'

No.5011 *Tintagel Castle* entering Box Tunnel with an up express. 'On my way to shop in Bath I often used to walk down the platelayers' embankment pathway to photograph trains at Box Tunnel.'

No.1024 *County of Pembroke* climbing Dauntsey incline. 'I had taken over the driving duties from Driver F Griffin and had opened the regulator to its maximum up the bank, after a stop at Dauntsey.' Photographed by Fireman Brian Boase.

Chapter 2

The Enginemen

Many times I have been asked the question: what sort of a man is Kenneth Leech? Often the questioner has seemed a trifle overawed, not only by reason of Kenneth's special place in the annals of British steam, (truly, he is a legend in his own time) but also because of his great age and the sagacity he brings to bear on the railway scene of yesteryear.

Always people are incredulous about the extent of his footplate experience. So many engines, so many trips, spanning almost two decades. How did he get away with it? How were the facts of what was going on down in the West Country kept from the hierarchy in Paddington?

I put questions such as these to Kenneth one afternoon as we sat sifting through hundreds of photographs.

'I reckon if you'd been caught it would have made newspaper headlines!' I teased. 'You'd never get away with it today.'

'No, I don't think I would,' he replied, gently. 'But you see in those days the management was prepared to turn a blind eye. 'You must, of course, take into account my professional record, and membership of the Institute of Locomotive Engineers made me pretty well-known.

'I also fancy my articles in leading railway magazines on official footplate trips made me appreciated. Also my practical experience on locos, both in England and France, made me recognised widely as an experienced and responsible person.'

Kenneth had, in fact, met the General Manager several times. On the second occasion the friend introducing him had said: 'Mr Leech rides about a lot on your engines,' and the general manager had replied: 'Yes, I know that, I've met him before.'

And so he had, on an official trip, when the General Manager had come up to the engine at Paddington and congratulated the crew on a remarkably fine trip up from Shrewsbury. Kenneth's friend was then moved to remark 'But, of course, you do a lot of footplating yourself!'

I agreed, Kenneth's credentials were most impressive, but even so, was not there an element of risk that some busy-body locomotive inspector or over-zealous station master might have reported him?

'Well, I didn't go into it with eyes closed' said Kenneth, patiently. 'In fact, I didn't set out with the intention of riding on the footplate. It all came about by chance, as a result of my taking photographs not only of locomotives, but of the enginemen, too. It was they who asked me to join them on the footplate.'

He explained how he had been careful never to be seen in places where he was not known. 'If ever I'd thought there was any risk of an engineman losing his job, I'd never have accepted an invitation. But I was well-known to several locomotive inspectors and occasionally rode with them. They told me they regarded me as a true railwayman, one of their own.'

Obviously, enginemen thought so, too, for never would they have allowed a bung-

Mrs Betty Martin on No.5025 *Chirk Castle.*'Mrs Martin, wife of a Westinghouse electrical engineer, was, surprisingly, wholeheartedly in love with GWR steam locomotives, especially Castles. Having photographed her in the cab of 5025, it occurred to me that, with luck, it might be possible to arrange a footplate trip for her.

'I tackled my best friend, Driver Bill Bateman, but as I had expected, he didn't like the idea at all, and took quite a bit of persuading. Finally, he agreed on condition that Betty dressed completely as a man, and that the trip would be between Bath & Chippenham after dark.

'Luckily, one of Bill's workings included such a turn with a Castle. I drove the disguised Betty to Bath by car, and saw her safely to the spot on the platform where Bill would stop to pick her up, and then went about half-way back to Chippenham where I had a good view of the line and could watch the train pass.

'It was clear that Bill was really punching the engine along as it went past me with the glow from the open firehole bright orange-yellow.

'Bill told me the next day that he had reached 75 mph before shutting off for the stop at Chippenham, and he could see that Mrs Martin was really thrilled through and through with enjoyment.

'I wonder has any other woman travelled as fast on a steam locomotive as did Betty Martin?'

No.7033 *Hartlebury Castle*. Driver Cyril Palmer (Old Oak Common) leaving Bristol Temple Meads on an up train (left). Driver Jack Lawes (Swindon) is on the 2-8-0 *Austerity*. 'Both drivers were good friends of mine. It was a million-to-one-chance I was able to photograph them simultaneously from a moving train.'

No.7033 *Hartlebury Castle*. Driver Cyril Palmer at Swindon, before doing the Swindon-Reading run start to stop in 34 minutes dead, including a slight check at Reading West. 'Cyril had done his very best to get me to ride with him, but I was not known at Reading, and felt it was too risky,though Cyril pleaded: 'Come on! I'd be prepared to lose my job for you!' 'I think I was wise to travel in the train. No.7033 reached speeds up to 90 mph. I knew the speedometer was a shade fast so timed it from my coach. Cyril put up a virtuoso performance to show me what I was missing!'

No.7033 *Hartlebury Castle*. Driver Bill Church, top-link, Old Oak Common. Appropriately, his fireman was named Ward! 'Bill had been on a gas turbine locomotive during a test for acceleration, taking a train from a standing start at the lowest point of Severn Tunnel. He said, he almost choked; and that was why he always dashed all-out at Box Tunnel with the gas turbine on an up train from Bath. He was afraid he might get stuck in the tunnel, and be overcome by fumes!'

No.5066 *Wardour Castle*. Cyril Palmer, top-link, Old Oak Common. 'I always was persuaded – No! – forced, to drive when I rode with Cyril!'

No.6000 *King George V*. SR Stewart's Lane driver Sam Gingell as a passenger (right), with Walter Harris, Old Oak Common, top-link driver. 'Sam enjoyed footplate trips so much he even took them on his days-off! He also rode on the footplate with my friend the legendary Driver Bill Hoole, on the East Coast main line.'

No.4707. Driver Herbert Lee and Driver Baker (Reading) and Driver Con Mason (Swindon) at Bath on 4 February 1959. 'Cold weather and a draughty cab! Note the extra high footplate of the *forty-seveners* and the low cab roof. I did not like these engines. They rode roughly, due to the Cartazzi trailing axlebox. One was always knocking one's head on the cabside! But they were very strong.'

No.2927 *Saint Patrick*. Driver Arthur Taylor at Bath 22 July 1950. A good cab view. Nice clean front and a good deep fire. Steam gauge on the mark – and a full boiler! 'Arthur Taylor gave me my very first footplate ride, at and around, Swindon Station on No. 2908 Lady of Quality in 1949.'

ling amateur to ride with them; which posed the question: what was the secret of Kenneth's empathy with drivers?

'Throughout my life I have never had any sense of social status. I felt enginemen were experienced and responsible, and always treated all grades as my equals, or, as regards their job, my superiors. But I think deep-down the real reason was because I was in love with steam engines, and to be an engineman had been my strong wish from a kid.'

Even so, I felt that this explanation went only some way to answering why anyone in his retirement years should of his own volition, day after day, hoist himself onto the footplate of a steam locomotive and bend to the back-breaking task of shovelling coal into a voracious furnace. Again I prompted Kenneth: what was his motivation over so many years? Was it an attempt to achieve perfection in the job? What kept his enthusiasm white hot at a time when most men of

his age would have been taking an afternoon nap?

'I enjoyed it thoroughly' he replied. 'Listening to music might have equalled it, but I couldn't find in Chippenham, the deep musical activities and friendships I had enjoyed in London before the Second War settled me in Chippenham. My other consuming interest – rock climbing – was a weekend joy.

'But in answer to your second question: Yes, I looked for perfection. I was expert on the job and loved the action. A Swindon driver once said to me, a few minutes after I'd started driving his engine for the first time. 'You know, you're a born engineman. You get on a strange engine and in less than half a mile you've found the best way to drive her.' That driver, by the way, was a Swindon J.P., and was granted special leave for his days on the Bench.'

But why did you never lose your enthusiasm? I persisted.

Suddenly, Kenneth grew tired of fencing with words and with a mischievous glint in his eyes he said, 'My wife, Gladys, she had the answer': 'Kenneth has never really grown up' she used to say.'

It is easy, of course, to suppose that the drivers were in some way flattered by Kenneth's interest in their job. At first they may have been mindful of his age and his status as a boss at Westinghouse, but they grew to know and love him (yes!) as a friend, and for many his trip with them was the highlight of their day and was looked forward to.

'Always I was greeted with a welcoming friendliness; a man to man attitude, perfectly free and easy. I have more than once been asked for my advice about whether to carry on or fail the engine for some not very important defect. They had probably already made up their minds, but seemed pleased and relieved that my judgement did happen to be the same as theirs in all instances.'

No.5905 *Knowsley Hall.* **Driver Fred Griffin and Fireman Blakemore − both Swindon. Fred was a great friend of the young enthusiasts who haunted Chippenham station.**

There was never any doubt as to who was the boss on the footplate. Physical appearance alone and the general demeanour of the man identified the driver of the locomotive. One can appreciate that the driver was quite happy to be elevated to the unofficial role of acting locomotive inspector when Kenneth temporarily took over, but one wonders if the fireman felt the same when he was made redundant for long periods.

'They liked it. Never any complaints. And very occasionally the fireman left the cab and sat down in the train!'

One time this proved awkward. Kenneth was firing to *City of Truro* alongside Driver Bill Bateman, when at Badminton Station in the dark it was found the headlamp had given out. 'Neither of us had a match,' Kenneth recalls, 'and Bill had to go into the train to rout out the fireman!'

The regularity with which Kenneth rode on the footplate is surprising, four, even five times a week, when possible, but 'only more or less on local trips.' There are photographs of him taken in the cab by enginemen where he is seen soberly attired in a trilby hat and a worn raincoat. He could easily have been taken for a railway official; for loco inspectors rarely, if ever, wore a proper uniform.

Neither did Kenneth have a black metal snap-box, the sort in which enginemen traditionally carried their bread and cheese, and bacon and eggs for frying on the shovel, with the daily running orders stowed away in a separate compartment in the lid. Rather, he would arrive at the station with a small attache case, the sort that might hold books or business papers. Only on the occasional 100 mile trip, or over, did he wear a conventional boilersuit.

Over many years, Kenneth Leech became known to top-link enginemen throughout the west of England, and was as well-spoken of in Old Oak Common as he was in his local Swindon and Bristol (Bath Road) loco sheds. He shared the footplate and the firing and driving with dozens of enginemen and finds little difficulty in giving an *identikit* description of a typical Great Western driver. But, firstly, it must be appreciated that a youngster joining the railway with ambitions of becoming a top-link driver could look ahead to many years of toil, first as a cleaner, then an as an apprentice fireman, and so on, working his way up at an agonisingly slow rate through the various links. Those fortunate enough to make the top grade would have spent some 15-20 years in the lower orders, so that when promotion to passenger work came they would most likely be well into their middle-forties.

To the travelling public engine drivers always appeared as fatherly figures. Never did they seem hurried or in any way agitated, and their demeanour inspired a feeling of confidence and well-being.

Often, at the end of a long journey when time had been kept to the very minute, well wishers would make their way down the platform to the head of the train to say thank you to the driver and his mate. And, of course, enginemen were always the doyens, the adventure book heroes, of small boys or *spotters* as they were popularly known.

Kenneth, however, draws a much more incisive and real picture of the denizens of the footplate, and recalls a typical driver as being of medium build, usually looking his age, or over, but not at all unhealthy. Invariably of smart appearance (overalls, of course) and giving the impression of being alert and feeling up to the job. He would most likely have a keen but quiet sense of humour, though his comments might often be sardonic, and his mood would vary with the job and the state of the engine. Very rarely would he betray a bad temper, only if compelled to take, or be booked, on a poor engine.

But were enginemen as a whole loyal to the railway? Keen on the job? Or was it merely a means to a weekly pay packet?

'They all felt proud and satisfied to be a GWR driver' said Kenneth. 'I never heard a grouse or even a mention about pay.'

But what of their private lives? Were enginemen sportsmen, gardeners, musicians, bookworms? Did they have an interest outside the railway?

'No, I don't recall any of them having hobby interests − except one and his was motorbikes! Essentially they were family men, but the whole of their working and sleeping hours − even their diet − was at the beck and call of the shift-work system. They were indeed true servants of the company: they had no time for outside pursuits.

'Not many lived to any great age, and this may well have been due to shift-work and long hours preventing most of them from having a hobby, and they had no interest thereafter.'

Driver Bill Bateman was almost unique

in living to 93. He was born and raised in Fishguard and joined the GWR at that depot. He spent his early years at Old Oak Common and elsewhere before moving to Swindon. It was Bill who persuaded Kenneth to take his first footplate trip. Sometimes, thereafter, Kenneth drove, but he much preferred firing to Bill's driving, particularly after dark.

Another good friend was Driver Jermey (Old Oak Common). He became so bored in retirement that he pocketed his pride and got a job as shop labourer in his old shed. On the other hand Tommy Worth, also a top-link engineman from Old Oak Common ('he always had a lighted pipe in his mouth') refused to drive diesels and packed in the job early, only to die soon after of cancer of the throat.

Driver Charlie Wasley was also most friendly. He was an ex- *Cheltenham Flyer* driver with great experience in maintaining high-speeds and keeping to close timings. Kenneth recalls one occasion, on the *Bristo-*

No.5547 *The Sorcerer's Apprentice*. 'When taking water at Bath(!) the water tank overflowed. Bill Bateman did not notice, but his fireman did. 'I recall we ran through Box Station at 70 mph on this trip.'

lian with No.6015 *King Richard III*, they ran three coaches past the stop signal at Slough. The signalman was to blame, and after the incident Charlie drove quite coolly but very fast to avoid a late arrival.

Often it is the minor incidents that come to mind most easily. As, for instance, the oil can that Driver 'Con' Mason left on the front bufferbeam at Chippenham, and which had not budged an inch on arrival at Bristol. It says a great deal for the smooth riding of the engine, or the regularity of the track, or a combination of the two!

Whilst Kenneth's firing and driving abilities were appreciated by the best enginemen, his skill as a photographer was also much acclaimed. Such was the regard for his prowess behind the lens and his skill in the dark room that 'Con' Mason insisted Kenneth should be the official photographer at his wedding. Driver Bert Potter was another good friend. He was well-known for having regularly driven the Royal Train. Once he was presented to Her Majesty Queen Elizabeth (now the Queen Mother) accompanied by the General Manager and Traffic Superintendent. Bert answered one of Her Majesty's questions with a sly dig at the officials,

which made The Queen laugh.

Perhaps the liveliest character of all was Driver Charlie Brown, he always seemed bubbling over with fun. Kenneth had photographed him a number of times and in return Charlie started dropping scribbled notes asking Kenneth to meet him on such and such an up train. He would then insist that Kenneth accept gifts of eggs and freshly-churned butter which he had acquired at Plymouth. 'I recall firing to Charlie Brown on 6013 when he deliberately 'caned' her beyond my firing capacity as a joke. He eased off as soon as I had given up.'

It might appear from these notes which focus almost entirely on the driver that Kenneth had little regard for the firemen. Not so; always he has maintained that firing is a man's job that required a great deal of practice and understanding of the idiosyncrasies of many different locomotives to make the job perfect. The driver being the senior of the two men was in charge of the engine and therefore Kenneth was on the footplate by his invitation alone. The time-honoured code of the railway deemed that the fireman should never usurp his driver's hard-earned seniority. He should know and respect his

place in the pecking order: one day his own time would come.

Of locomotive inspectors, Chief Inspector Charlie Pullen clearly held his place on the 'other side of the fence' as a senior professional. Although he was friendly in his dealings with Kenneth he maintained a degree of reserve and was addressed always as 'Mister' Pullen, never Charlie. On the other hand, Chief Inspector Bill Andress was a personal friend with a true sense of humour. In a letter to Kenneth he wrote: 'I have just been on a tour around every loco depot and asked at each if they knew you. The answer was, 'of course', in every case, and I began to think you were better known than I was!'

Another time, after Kenneth had spent an evening at Swindon, Bill Andress accompanied him to the station and said to the driver of the down train waiting in the bay. 'Mr Leech will be riding with you to Chippenham. Goodbye, Kenneth.'

Always it was Kenneth and Bill. A relationship expressed in a friendly, chafing spirit, bright with good humour. Kenneth was invited to Paddington to attend and even to say a few words at the official pres-

No.6015 *King Richard III*. Down *Bristolian* 19 May 1958. 'When I took this photograph, Tony Tyler was a top-link fireman to Charlie Wasley at Old Oak Common. He subsequently became a driver, then a loco inspector and a driving instructor, and finally, the inspector in charge of the Royal Train. He had a keen sense of humour. On one occasion, as a fireman, he allowed the King he was on to blow-off a head of steam when I was chatting to his driver in Bath Station. Naturally, I put in a goading remark about inefficient firemen allowing their engines to blow-off unnecessarily. Tony at once chipped in: 'Well, we're not accustomed to stopping at wayside stations!'

No.7032 *Denbigh Castle*. Driver Bert Giles (Temple Meads, Bristol) on No. 7032, 3 April 1959, the last day before his retirement. 'Bert was probably the best-known top-link driver at Bristol, most likely because of his record of keeping good time, and being chosen for many special jobs.'

No.5963 *Wimpole Hall*. 'Running into Dauntsey Station. The gauge reading shows that I was making a gentle stop.'

No.7037 *Swindon*. Driver 'George' (Alf) Guyatt (Swindon). 'It was said, probably in fun, that at his wedding service Alf pulled out of his pocket a piece of GWR cotton waste, and wiped his hands on it!'

No.1025 *County of Radnor*. Driver Sid Davies and Fireman Davy Jones – both Swindon. 'Sid was a thoroughly good-hearted chap with a keen sense of humour. Why he chose to look so fierce when this photo was taken, I don't know!'

entation to Bill Andress on his retirement.

Other inspectors were always friendly, perhaps because they knew they would not have to keep an eye on Kenneth, as they would do for a stranger riding officially with them.

'Inspector Hancock, particularly, in the very last days of steam, thought of me and most kindly arranged a trip on the 4.15 pm ex-Paddington, on 7029 *Thornbury Castle*, the very last steam-hauled express, and encouraged the driver to run up to and hold 90 mph en route to Banbury.'

Although enginemen were responsible for Kenneth's remarkable footplate record, he is mindful of an 'engineman' of another kind who made possible all his photographs of locomotives in Swindon Works.

Stan Morris was foreman of Boilers and Stationary Engines at Swindon Works, responsible among other duties for seeing that locos arriving for repairs were made ready to enter the repair shop. When the work on the engine was completed it would be coupled to its tender with water and coal enough for its trial trip, oiled, and sent over to the running shed.

When No. 6022 *King Edward III* got the first 4-row superheater, Kenneth Cook, then Works Manager, invited Kenneth to come to the Works and photograph the engine before it went into service. It was then that Kenneth met Stan Morris for the first time.

'Stan Morris put 6022 into position and after taking photos I asked him to put a Hall for me to photograph. Later he got a pannier tank from the running shed, put me on it and took me to my platform on Swindon Station.'

Stan kept in touch with Kenneth and soon he was placing up to three repaired and repainted engines in suitable positions for him to photograph on a Sunday morning.

'Usually there was no one about – though once Stan and I encountered Mr Smeddle (the last steam C.M.E.) himself! Luckily he had recently told me I would be welcome at the Works anytime I wished to visit them, and I used this in my surprise talk with him, and he let it go.

'So, you see, I owe a big number of my photographs of locos in mint condition to Stan Morris. We became good friends and after he had retired spent several lineside summer days together at Whiteball and Savernake.'

But for his great empathy with enginemen, inspectors and officialdom, in general, throughout the Western Region Kenneth Leech's unofficial footplate career could never have blossomed in the way that it did. And, certainly, without the likes of Stan Morris and the acquiescence of the Swindon Works management many of his historic locomotive portraits would never have been possible.

Kenneth remains overwhelmingly grateful to all the many friends of years long gone; but with the end of steam and the coming of the age of the diesel it was the turn of the enginemen to pay him a personal tribute. Unfortunately, Kenneth was unable to attend a dinner in his honour at Bristol (Bath Road) but was chief guest at similar events held at the Old Oak Common and Swindon depots.

It was the end of the line. The joyride, alas, was over.But not quite. For even now, more than thirty years on, the memories of those stirring days burn as a bright beacon in the lively mind of this remarkable centenarian. And the words of his friend Driver Bill Bateman echo down the tunnel of time...'You'll never die – they'll have to shoot you!'

No.5322. 'I rode with Bill Bateman more than any other driver (130 trips) sometimes driving, more often than not firing. I enjoyed firing as a relaxation, whereas driving was always a great responsibility for me.' Bill Bateman died in 1989 at the age of 93.

No.5034 *Corfe Castle*. Driver Bert Potter was well-known as the driver of the Royal Train. On his retirement he was introduced to Queen Elizabeth the present Queen Mother. He was the driver who put No. 6015 *King Richard III* (with a double-chimney) up to 108 mph. This was on the *Cornish Riviera Limited* with test engineers on the footplate, timing the performance.

No.5056 *Earl of Powis*. Driver Frank Gleed, Old Oak Common. 'Frank always let me drive, but sometimes I did the firing; whenever I felt like it, in fact!'

No.6000 *King George V* emerging from Dainton Tunnel with the down *Cornish Riviera Limited*, on 6 June 1957. 'I was wearing goggles, for the cinders from the chimney were bouncing down from the tunnel roof like hailstones!'

Chapter 3
Footplate Experiences

The personalities of enginemen have already been discussed. And in 'Portraits of Castles' (Moorland 1981) Kenneth has set down his footplate experiences in considerable detail. However, in this latest work he has been encouraged to look back over almost four decades, and this verbatim, account of our various discussions, I believe, adds a further useful and interesting dimension to the fund of knowledge he has bequeathed to posterity.

Kenneth has always let it be known that driving a steam engine took second place to his love of firing. 'To pick up the shovel and relieve the fireman for part of the journey was a joy.' He has said that driving an engine on a good trip was delightful, but it was not a *pure* delight, for niggling at the back of his mind was the continuous feeling of responsibility, and the need to do everything perfectly.

Therefore, I chose to discuss his firing experiences first of all, and warmed to the subject, as it were, by asking if he built the fire differently for each class of locomotive.

'Always the same sort of fire,' he replied, 'relatively thin but well alight at the front of the firebox, gradually deepening towards the firehole end, where the main depth of coal would be well alight and burning brightly, but the top layer of coal would not be fully burning. This helped to keep the footplate cool — and the driver's shins, too!

'But the depth of fire I kept — or tried to keep — depended on how hard the engine was being worked. Of course, if the fire was seriously dirty or clinkered, special firing variations would probably be necessary, and if there happened to be a considerable amount of mileage ahead, then one would go through the fire with at least the pricker and probably the dart breaking up the clinker, which would have to be picked up and thrown out using the clinker shovel. But always I left that to the fireman!

'Back in 1913, as a young fireman on the London Tilbury and Southend Railway I had daily to 'clean the fire' at least once on each trip — breaking up the clinker with the dart, throwing out the debris with the 8 or 9 foot long clinker shovel — all this usually, but not invariably, on the shed and raking the fire level with the rake when actually running the train.

'I was, therefore, forced to realise at 60 years of age it was a part of the fireman's job I could not tackle. But I was able to use a shovel until the end of steam in service — though, alas, not nowadays!'.

Kenneth found that all classes of engine were relatively easy to fire and to make steam, except the Kings. This may have been due partly to his being getting on for sixty years of age when he started firing GWR steam locomotives in service — 'King fireboxes were just too long to be easy for me to fire,' he recalls.

His longest spell on the shovel was from Paddington to Reading, with a heavy train well over the Castle's permitted load. A

No.6000 *King George V* **with the down** *Cornish Riviera Limited* **at Parsons Cliff, Dawlish, on 6 June 1957.**

No.5085 *Evesham Abbey*. Start and Finish.
'The first picture (above) was taken from the train behind 5085 on the 11.45am ex-Temple Meads, Bristol. The second picture (right) shows the same train arriving in Paddington.'

No.5027 *Farleigh Castle*. From the footplate of No. 5027 on the 1.15 pm Paddington to Bristol express, approaching Cholsey at 70 mph. Each of the two freight trains is headed by a 28xx Class 2-8-0 locomotive.

similar experience was, again, on a Castle, from Swindon, firing sufficient coal to get the 14-coach train to Bristol.

Kenneth recalls — 'I could not have carried on much longer on the first trip, but there were stops at Chippenham and Bath on the second, and I think I could have carried on more or less indefinitely without being exhausted, but with the relief of the longish idle periods between each spell of firing.'

But often it was the type and quality of coal that made all the difference between a good or a bad trip. In the earlier years coal was usually of a consistently good quality, but towards the end it was often a mixture of synthetic briquettes and dust, and very little joy to fire, compared with the original Welsh coal of the GWR. Even so, there were often large lumps of coal in the tender which took some very hard knocks to break up to firing size, as well as needing care to avoid making slack.

Certainly Kenneth could not match a regular fireman in terms of weight of coal per shovelful or speed of firing. He could manage around 12lbs of coal, firing to the front of the firebox, but strong, young firemen would pick up well over 20lbs on each shovelful and seemed to be able to send it with no particular effort to the front of a King's firebox.

At the age of 68, on an epic run, he fired about 60lbs a minute for some 40 minutes, which compares with a firing rate of between 70-80lbs a minute for a young professional.

'They could go on like that for long periods', says Kenneth. 'Firemen had little competition from me! Even in my youth on the London and Tilbury the normal fire would not have raised steam if fired in any other than moderate shovelsful. This would be some 6 to 8 shovelsful at a time, repeating the process after about a minute's respite.'

At sixty, did Kenneth's muscles ache, or did regular firing keep him in trim like a trained athlete?

'In spite of my age, I was fit enough not to have any aches or pains after any firing trips.' he replied.....Remarkable.

This poses the question: were firemen, despite their youth, prone to back problems — lumbago, arthritis and suchlike? 'Not in my perhaps limited experience', says Kenneth, 'while they were still regularly firing.

'But some drivers did find their backs a bit on the stiff side as they grew older, and this may have been a relic of their firing days — or possibly a reminder of work on their allotment!'

Firing a locomotive imposed a physical strain, but driving a steam engine demanded a continuous alertness and induced a mental fatigue that was truly tiring in the long run. A sense of responsibility and awareness was also constant, particularly in observing the signalled right of way and the clearness of the track ahead: there was a need to be prepared for all eventualities from stray animals and fallen obstacles to trespassers and children playing dangerous games on the

No.6018 *King Henry VI* running into Bath Station on 22 May 1958. 'Note the signal cabin raised well above the platform canopy. I took a number of head-on photographs of trains from this vantage point.'

No. 7036 *Taunton Castle* **approaching Bath on 7 September 1963.** 'Two days after this photograph was taken, No. 7036 was withdrawn for breaking-up, while still in perfect condition.'

No.6012 *King Edward VI* with the down Paddington to Plymouth express Crookwood, 25 July 1961.

line.

Asked for an appraisal of a skilful driver, Kenneth was at pains to point out that driving varied with the engine and the job. No two engines, although of the same class, were exactly similar in their behaviour, so that the skilful driver would try to get the 'feel' of the engine and adjust the regulator and cut-off. 'A good driver would never drive his engine too hard, always driving in the most economical way and nursing his charge, if it was shy for steam. He would keep an unseen eye on how his fireman was faring, keep intermediate timing without recourse to his watch, and finally know all about the variations of the road, and almost subconsciously adapt to them, while at the same time he would always be aware of how the engine was liking and responding to his calls on it.'

And a poor driver?

'I can't say I came across many poor drivers', said Kenneth. 'The long years of apprenticeship and waiting for promotion sorted the good from the bad. But, if pressed, I would say, I think a poor driver was one who drove unnecessarily hard – thrashed his engine – was on bad terms with his mates and fairly obviously did not enjoy the work, but 'got by' with it.'

As we have seen Kenneth was already an experienced enginemen when he began working on Great Western engines. He had been used to making accurate and time-saving stops on the Tilbury line of his youth, and at first put his method of making station stops into practice on the GWR, but very soon was told that he should make gentler stops which would not upset (in any way!) the passengers. And so he tried never to reduce the train pipe vacuum from 25 inches to below 15 inches, and thereafter took care to stick to this method.

He regards his proudest moment, finest achievement – call it what you will – arriving in Reading Station after firing a Castle from Paddington on the 1.00pm with a load far over the limit for the engine, and getting ahead of booked time, so that he had to come almost to a stand at Reading East signals. 'And I kept the steam pressure up to the blowing-off point all the way' he said proudly. 'But the fireman attended to the boiler water level for me, because I never came off the shovel.'

Kenneth's worst driving experience goes back to the early years on the Tilbury line on a down train with a driver who had let him drive while he fired.

He asked me: 'Was Laindon distant off?' And then I realised with a start that through culpable negligence I had missed seeing it. I felt even worse, as he was a driver whom I was very fond of, 'Dumps' Stephens. But he let me continue and I was too selfish and idiotic not to hand over the regulator to him in shame.

'But this lapse cured me an I can truthfully say that never again have I missed a signal.'

It is, perhaps, a hangover from this singular experience that made Kenneth ex-

No.6012 *King Edward VI* with the up Plymouth to Paddington non-stop express, approaching Parson and Clerk Tunnel, Dawlish, 26 July 1961.

tremely cautious driving at high speeds. He claims a fastest run of about 85 miles an hour down Dauntsey Bank, but says that he felt, even at lower speeds than this, the distance from first sighting the distant signal was too short to be sure of stopping the train before the home signal, if it had been against him.

'I must say none of the drivers I had ridden with seemed to worry about this point, though it was true that only on the down Bristolian, with its two sections ahead always kept clear did drivers reckon to exceed 85 miles an hour 'down Dauntsey'.

'One very experienced driver of my acquaintance actually shut off steam at the top of Dauntsey Bank and thereafter rolled all the way to a stop at Chippenham Station without opening the regulator.'

As a counterpoint to my question on skilful driving I asked Kenneth what he regarded as being perfect driving conditions: 'First of all, both enginemen feeling happy. Next, an engine in at least reasonably good condition and steaming freely on good coal. The job should be a relatively easy one for engine and crew, and the fire clean and bright all over.

'And finally, that the train was well on time, and had plenty of coal and water, and the injectors were not tricky to get at to operate.'

Kenneth was as happy on a freight engine as on a King or a Castle and he rode them in most weathers, by day or by night, in winter and summer.

In summer he recalls that tank engines could be trying in the heat of the cab and so could Britannia's and other BR types. But GWR tender engines did not really bother him. It was, of course, cold and draughty in winter both on tank and tender engines. 'But one got pretty well used to it, and of course opening the firehole door could be a real help, though not a cure.'

Kenneth was never in charge of a locomotive in heavy snow or fog. And in driving rain he chose to pick up the shovel and fire. 'I always tried to keep clear of driving in bad weather. I felt sure the driver would prefer me not to drive – even if he had made the offer, one could tell.'

Ask him what he remembers about night journeys and Kenneth is likely to recall the rainbow in the steam as it drifted through the white glare of the open firebox. But soon he is talking practicalities, such as green signal lights being less visible than red; and the fact that the signals level with an overbridge behind them were much harder to discern.

Not surprisingly, Kenneth grew to know the 'road' on certain stretches of track extremely well. He was particularly familiar with Bath to Swindon, and also from Trowbridge to Swindon. 'Well, enough for the normal weather conditions, but never really well enough to think I should be at home in serious fog.'

Talking with Kenneth about his years on the footplate is a stimulating experience. He is as enthusiastic today as though it had all happened yesterday, although he makes frequent reference to his log book, which still preserves the coal dust between its well thumbed pages.

For Kenneth Leech life has never been a chore. He approaches each day with an enthusiasm for living and the enjoys sharing his interests with others.

'I have found over a large number of years, that not only enginemen, but inspectors, station staff – including station masters – signalmen and almost all railwaymen during the Steam Age, were friendly and good humoured, while being always concerned with the matter of safety most of all.'

A fine tribute to the men of the Great Western from a true enthusiast whom time will not forget.

No.6012 *King Edward VI* with the Plymouth to Paddington non-stop express, passing through Burlescombe between Exeter and Taunton, 26 July 1961. Note the almost *invisible* signal.

No.6012 *King Edward VI* approaching Exeter, St David's, on a Plymouth to Paddington non-stop express, 26 July 1961.

No.6012 *King Edward VI* with the Plymouth to Paddington non-stop express at Heywood Road, 26 July 1961. 'Here we ran into a layer of bad coal and at the same time part of the brick arch collapsed. We were in trouble for steam for a few miles'.

No.6000 *King George V* heading the down *Cornish Riviera Limited*, running over Crookwood viaduct, 6 June 1957.

No.6027 *King Richard I* with the down *Cornish Riviera* at Somerton, sometime in 1953.

The Named Expresses

Although Kenneth Leech photographed dozens of 'named' expresses, the only ones that he got to know really well were the *Cornish Riviera Limited* and the *Bristolian*. He rode twice on the footplate of the down *Riviera*, but had a great deal more to do with the *Bristolian*. There was good reason why he did not enjoy more footplate excursions on these two, for both trains were crack expresses and therefore had tight running schedules to maintain and were always under the close scrutiny of the signalling and operating staff of the railway. It was thought best that Kenneth should confine his cab-work to less prestigious runs rather than risk high-profile appearances that might have raised awkward questions in high places. Footplate passes were not normally granted on the *Bristolian*, but Kenneth received an official letter with his pass for the down *Bristolian* pointing this out, but saying that an exception was being made in his case.

Kenneth recalls that on one of his *Riviera* runs the rostered King failed and a standby Hall took-over the duty. Although the task should have been well within the capacity of the Hall it, nevertheless, proved a very tiring day's work for the fireman, struggling for most of the way with a dirty fire and a badly run-down engine. The locomotive steamed well only intermittently, and after three and a half hours of continuous firing the fireman was worn out. This was on a down trip and Kenneth feels that the up journey may have been a bit easier, but never having ridden on the up *Riviera* he is reluctant to give an opinion.

The Cornish Riviera Limited

The *Cornish Riviera Limited* was born in July 1904 and until 1926 was famous as being the longest non-stop railway run in the world, first halt North Road Station, Plymouth, a distance of some 226 miles west and southward of Paddington.

The early part of the *Riviera* run was smooth and relatively gentle as the engine got into its stride with a load of some 500 tons behind the tender, including a full complement of passengers and luggage. By Slough speed would most likely have been touching 70 mph, and at Aldermaston the engine would have topped-up with water from the troughs between the rails (the water softening plant here was the first of its kind in the country) for the steady climb ahead, reaching Savernake Summit, near Hungerford, at around 11.45 am, an hour and a quarter after leaving London.

Savernake was a favourite haunt of Kenneth's, a place where he photographed locomotives working hard up the 1 in 184 gradient, *collar-work* as it was called. But once over the summit the pace rapidly increased on the glorious racing stretch down to Westbury, touching 80 mph while descending the 1 in 220 from Patney to Lavington. Past Taunton and the train would begin the stiff ascent to Whiteball Summit (another of Kenneth's favourite vantage points) the last three miles before

No.6004 *King George III* with the down *Cornish Riviera* diverted because of engineering works, on 9 May 1954, approaching Chippenham.

No.6010 *King Charles I* is steaming well at the top of the stiff climb up to Whiteball Summit.

No.6008 *King James II* at Cole with the down *Cornish Riviera Limited*, just about to pass under the Somerset & Dorset Railway bridge. Trains at this point were usually running easily down the bank.

No.6015 *King Richard III* heading the up *Cornish Riviera Limited* at Whiteball, just below the summit of the climb, on 28 July 1956. The engine is fitted with the first type of double chimney, and is working well with 14 on.

the tunnel increasing from a formidable figure of 1 in 90 to an even stiffer 1 in 81. Interestingly, one end of the 1092 yards long Whiteball Tunnel is in Somerset the other in Devon.

Whiteball was virtually the boundary line of Kenneth's photographic sorties, anything further afield being usually undertaken as a footplate ride. The *Cornish Riviera Limited* was undoubtedly one of his favourite expresses and features in many of his photographs.

The train was steam-hauled into the early 1960's and after that its aura sadly faded. Its *Limited* title was dropped in 1977, and in 1979 it became one of the railway's new breed of Inter-City 125 Highspeed Trains (HST). Sadly, the famous headboard, once carried on the smokebox of so many renowned steam engines, is now but a museum artefact, the name *Cornish Riviera* surviving only as a paper label stuck onto carriage windows.

The Bristolian

The London to Bristol and return express, *The Bristolian*, in comparison to the *Cornish Riviera Limited*, might have been considered a modern-day introduction. The train entered service on 9 September 1935 to commemorate the centenary of the Great Western Railway and the City of Bristol's historic association with the railway.

The double journey of 236 miles (weekdays only) began in London (Paddington) at 8.45am and ran via Bath, returning from Bristol at 4.30 pm via Badminton. The service was suspended from the outbreak of war in 1939 and was not restored to the timetable until 1951. In 1960 *The Bristolian* name was superseded by *The Blue Pullman* which ran until 1973.

Kenneth Leech had more to do with the *Bristolian* than the *Riviera* and regularly exchanged observations on the performance of the locomotives which were chosen to work

this high-flyer. He recalls that with a Castle in good condition and with good coal it was not a trying trip for the crew, in physical terms. However, the onus was on the driver to keep up to the mark on timing and the signalmen had permanent orders to keep two sections clear ahead of the express, and this made the driver more confident and happy in maintaining the high speeds which were demanded of him.

As regards the work on the footplate, Kenneth feels it was quite a normal job for the fireman, and not too worrying for the driver, provided the engine chosen for the job was in good shape and burning good coal. So much so, that the authorities made tests on one or two occasions to cut the journey time from 105 minutes to 95 minutes, including two arranged delays on route, each costing 5 minutes, one after Didcot to 15 mph, for about a mile, and another 15 mph slack down Dauntsey Bank, when normally 85-95 mph would have been held.

No.7018 *Drysllwyn Castle*. No.7018 races through Hullavington at 95 mph on 21 June 1956. Note the double chimney, but with 3-row superheater not the final 4-row version. The chimney is sheet metal, later replaced in cast iron.

No.5040 *Stokesay Castle* speeding through Hullavington Station at around 90 mph.

'I always liked No.5040, and had twelve trips on her of which I drove on six occasions and fired on three. Although she seemed a very good engine, the reverser was slightly incorrectly set, so that she showed 18 per cent on the indicator, whereas her performance and the small amount of noise and fuss she made were equivalent to 15-16 per cent on most other Castles.

No.6000 *King George V* on the up *Bristolian* passing Little Somerford at 85 mph on 29 July 1954. Driver A J Jones and Chief Inspector Pullen are on the footplate. King's were originally deployed on the 'Up', but Castles took over when it was found that they could do the job easily enough, if steaming normally.

No.6007 *King William III* on 21 July 1955 one mile east of Hullavington, about 100 yards from the Chippenham to Malmesbury road which runs under the railway.

No.5060 *Earl of Berkley*. '5060 was an Old Oak Common engine, and I took the photograph at Langley Crossing on 12 March 1958. She was running at about 80 mph. I had seven trips on her, three driving, three firing and one just as an observer.'

No. 6018 *King Henry VI* **with the down** *Bristolian* **on 28 July 1955 racing through Dauntsey at 102 mph. 'A friend of mine was on the train and had had a private word with the driver at Paddington! I'm told speed was held at 100 for 2 miles.'**

No.6002 *King William IV* heading the down *Merchant Venturer*, approaching Chippenham Station on 6 May 1953.

No.6024 *King Edward I*. 'The Spotters'. A delightful picture which captures the power and majesty of steam and the wonder and excitement of youth. It was taken on 25 August 1955 at Chippenham Station, down side, just east of the passenger platforms with the goods shed in background.

A King locomotive was used for these test runs, but although time was kept, it was felt that keen enginemen might be inclined to exceed various limits elsewhere, to make up lost time, and the idea was dropped. The normal double trip Temple Meads – Paddington – Temple Meads, was not considered by crews as anything to make a fuss about. And the fact that, in the event of engine failure, a Hawksworth Hall was able to make up most of the time lost on changing engines with a Castle en route and do the trip, finishing in perfect condition – as a thorough examination made before the Hall was allowed in service again proved the point.

The *Bristolian* on Mondays and Fridays was made up of eight bogies, seven the other three days, when a Castle was used; but normally a King was rostered on Mondays on the down trip. If there was no Castle available at Temple Meads for the up trip, a Hall was very occasionally used, but allowed an extra 10 minutes for the trip. Kenneth has no record of how these *freak trips* (as he calls them) worked, but on one occasion when he took photographs at Hullavington the speed of the Hall was much lower than the normal Castle speed.

As regards speeds, Castles seemed nearly always, on an up train, to be faster through Hullavington than Kings. On the down train, speeds through Chippenham were never as fast as might have been expected, due, Kenneth was told by several enginemen, to the drivers not liking the slight curve on the over-bridge just west of the station.

The Castle which attained the highest recorded speed on the up *Bristolian* was No 7032 Denbigh Castle, at about 102 mph at Little Somerford. But it was No 7018 Drysllwyn Castle which made the fastest overall time on the up train, on one particular day, with 7 coaches, then next day equalled the overall time with the 8 coach load; both trips were with the same Bath Road (Bristol) driver Jimmy Russe. However, it is unofficially recorded that on the down train, one or two Kings, with especially honoured re-cipients of footplate passes on board, reached or slightly exceeded 100 mph at Dauntsey.

The Merchant Venturer

The train which eventually became the *Merchant Venturer* was originally the 11.15 am from Paddington to Bath, Bristol and Weston-Super-Mare. It was given its titled headboard in 1951, as one of the Festival of Britain trains. The train was named after the ancient and historic Bristol Society of Merchant Venturers, and the time allowance for the non-stop run to Bath was 113 minutes, an average speed of 56.7 mph for the 106.9 miles start to stop.

Kenneth's photographs of the *Merchant Venturer* were specifically taken to catch driver friends on the footplate. Usually he photographed the down train as it sped through Chippenham at speeds of upto 70 mph.

The enginemen were from Old Oak Common, and generally well-known to Ken-

No.46237 *City of Bristol* seen working *The Merchant Venturer*, Bristol to London express, near Chippenham on 23 April 1955. The Duchess Pacific was brought in from the London Midland Region for a month's trial to compare performances with the Kings . This resulted in the Kings being fitted with double chimneys to improve their performances. In January 1956 the entire King Class was temporarily withdrawn due to fractures on the bogie frame on some of the class. Other LMR 4-6-2s loaned on this occasion were Nos.46207 *Princess Arthur of Connaught*, 46210 *Lady Patricia*, 46254 *City of Stoke on Trent* and 46257 *City of Salford*. These locomotives also worked Paddington – Wolverhampton at the same period.

No.7011 *Banbury Castle* and **7004***Eastnor Castle* behind. 'I captured this fine shot of two Castles working the 11.15 am *Merchant Venturer* about half-a-mile east of Chippenham one day in June 1953. Most likely, one of the engines was working 'home' to Bath Road, Bristol.'

No.4062 *Malmesbury Abbey* with the up *Merchant Venturer* at Thingley on 5 June 1952. 'This was a Castle job, but the renowned railway enthusiast and writer O.S.Nock (who was on the footplate) persuaded the authorities to allow a Star to work the train. 4062 did the job perfectly, I was told; and another Star, No. 4056 *Princess Margaret*, was put on the morning up train, and again did a first-class job.

The Stars were in decline when first I began to take a special interest in photographing Great Western engines. I rode on only three of them, the third and last being 4056 on 13 October 1955. The engine had recently had her last general repair in Swindon and was in perfect condition.

'It was then that top-link driver Bill Brown was moved to remark that 4056 was the best 'Castle' they had on Bristol, Bath Road Shed. An illustration of how very little margin of performance there was betweeen Stars and Castles.'

No.7034 *Ince Castle* on a *Merchant Venturer* at Thingley. Driver Bill Brown and his mate are looking out of the cab by prior arrangement with Kenneth.

No.7033 *Hartlebury Castle* with a down train approaching Chippenham. Note Calne branch points going off to the right.
   '7033 was a notably good Castle, but her speedometer read a bit fast and may have given enginemen a slightly too favourable impression.'

No.6012 *King Edward VI*. Down *Royal Duchy* at Savernake, sometime in July 1959, just east of the station. 'I had a number of good trips on 6012, but recall one on the down *Cornish Riviera* where she failed for steam at Reading, through a boiler-washer failing to secure a spark arresting baffle after 6012 was 'washed-out' the previous day.

neth. On the up return working (5.25 pm ex-Bristol) the train would make a number of additional stops on the way to Paddington, and sometimes Kenneth would photograph the down train with a view to a probable footplate trip on the return working.

The *Merchant Venturer* was often a long and heavy train, around 450 tons with passengers and luggage. It was renowned also for the lavish provision of dining accommodation.

On the down working the most likely class of motive power was a King, and on the return a Castle. The *Merchant Venturer* was withdrawn in 1965.

The Royal Duchy

Another named express which engaged Kenneth's attention from time to time was the *Royal Duchy*. The working from Paddington to Penzance was introduced in 1957, and enjoyed only a short life of eight years, being discontinued in 1965. The grandiose title *Royal Duchy*, needed the consent of Her Majesty The Queen. But as with *The Merchant Venturer*, Kenneth had little interest in the train other than the fact that Old Oak Common enginemen would be on the footplate. He recalls a particular occasion when he travelled to Westbury: 'Because Driver Harry Jermey had agreed to look out for me on the fireman's side. It was his last trip before retirement. Unfortunately, he forgot, and sailed past in grand style without taking his final curtain!'

No.5020 *Llantilio Castle* with the down *Royal Duchy* approaching Heywood Road junction.
'This was the last run of a well-known Old Oak Common top-link driver, Harry Jermey, before his retirement. I had arranged for him to put his head outside the cab for the photograph. Unfortunately, Harry forgot!'

No.5028 *Llantilio Castle* at Whiteball on 23 July 1955 with a down *Torbay Express*. The safety valve is blowing-off after the stiff climb up the bank.

No.7000 *Viscount Portal* at Whiteball, sometime in August 1954, with a down *Torbay Express*.

No.5074 *Hampden* leaving Paddington on the 9.55 am Pullman on 14 July 1955. Photographed from the window of the 8.26am up train from Chippenham, as it ran into Paddington four minutes early.

No.6853 *Morehampton Grange* on a running-in turn, stopping at Melksham station.
'I had driven the engine and stopped with it clear of the platform, jumped off the footplate, taken this picture and nipped back on to the footplate just in time to obey the guard's signal to start the train again.'

Chapter 5

The Locomotives

Ask Kenneth Leech if he has a favourite Great Western engine and he will most surely reply: 'Yes, of course, 2908 *Lady of Quality*. Her name fascinated me the moment I clapped eyes on her one evening at Chippenham Station.'

However, the engine that first kindled his photographic enthusiasm and ultimately set him off on his remarkable footplate adventures was another Saint, No.2945 *Hillingdon Court*. Again, it was at Chippenham on a 5.00 pm running-in turn from Swindon to Bristol, and he was struck by her smart appearance and the way she moved off so majestically into the evening sun.

But it was Lady of Quality that takes pride of place as the first Saint that Kenneth actually drove, for although he had arranged a footplate ride, he was surprised to be invited on the spur of the moment to take over the controls, although closely observed by the regular engineman.

Years later, when 2908 was about to be scrapped, he bought one of her nameplates and for many years it held pride of place on a wall in his railway room.

Not for aesthetic reasons only were Saint's his favourites. As a top-ranking engineer, Kenneth saw them as the finest achievement of George Jackson Churchward's 19-year span as Swindon's locomotive supremo. For it was with the introduction of the 2-cylinder 'Lady's', soon to be joined by 'Saints' and 'Courts' that the man regarded as the father of Great Western 4-6-0s set the design parameters which were to keep GWR locomotives in the forefront of steam traction in terms of speed, power and reliability for the next three decades.

It was during Kenneth Leech's impressionable youth, as an apprentice engineer with the London, Tilbury and Southend Railway, that Churchward reached the zenith of his genius. The keyword of the Great Western was 'standardization', not only in locomotive types, but in parts, too. Interchangeability of boilers, for example, between several classes of locomotive saw big cost-savings in engine repair and maintenance, and cut drastically the time an engine might be out of service.

As a young man he also witnessed the introduction of superheating, together with such refinements as top-feed to boilers. Water softening plants, which reduced heavy lime scaling in locomotive boilers, also appeared on the railway scene — and water troughs between the tracks from which water could be scooped at speed made long non-stop journeys possible.

Stirring years indeed!

Following hard on the heels of the Saints, the 4-cylinder Stars made their appearance in 1907-8. But whilst the Saints continued to run virtually unchanged for the next fifty or so years, the Star class after 1923 became decimated as many of its engines were withdrawn and replaced by Castles, or else modified and upgraded to Castle class status — yet another tribute to the flexibility of

No.2920 *Saint David*. **It is October 1953 and No.2920 the last of Churchward's renowned Saint class stands forlornly outside Swindon Works while the decision to save or scrap her is debated. By this time her main frames were loose, where they joined the front section of the bar framing, and some bolts were missing. The fervour of preservation had not yet gripped the railway fraternity and cold economic logic prevailed. There was no reprieve!**

No.2927 *Saint Patrick*. Seen here in pristine condition at Chippenham in February 1950 No.2927 was newly out of works and heading the 5.00 pm ex-Swindon running-in turn. She was condemned in December 1951.

No.2936 *Cefntilla Court* still in the plain green Great Western livery, is seen at Bath in September 1950. She was based at Cardiff for most of her working life, which ended in April 1951.

No.2937 *Clevedon Court* outside Swindon Works in June 1953, before her final journey to the scrapyard.

Churchward's standardization scheme.

The Stars were already a vanishing race when Kenneth began to take a special interest in Great Western engines in the late 'fifties, and he rode on only three. He reckons they were probably the best proportioned engines ever built, the cylinders, piston valves, wheels and boiler all perfectly matched.

But for sheer pleasure of driving he puts Castles at the top of his list. 'Full of vigour, responsive to regulator and cut-off, and usually free-steaming.'

Following Churchward's retirement his deputy, C B Collett, took over the hot seat, and in late 1923 the prototype locomotive of the new Castle class emerged from Swindon in the shape of No. 4073 *Caerphilly Castle*.

Whilst Castles were in direct lineage to the Stars, their larger cylinders, supplied with power from a boiler capable of generating steam at a pressure of 225 lbs psi, boosted tractive effort from the 27,800 lbs psi to 31,625 lbs psi.

Castles soon got into their full stride and locomotives of the class regularly hauled the *Cheltenham Flyer*, which daily performed the fastest non-stop run in the British Isles covering the 77 miles from Swindon to Paddington at an average speed of more than a mile per minute.

Kenneth's remarkable record included 757 trips on 149 different Castles. He drove 345 times, fired on another 301 and during that time photographed all 171 engines. 'They were superb machines', he recalls, 'capable of hauling enormous loads at high speeds, yet relatively low on coal and water consumption. And another thing about them', he adds with a chuckle, 'they had tip-up seats for the driver and the fireman!'

Four years after the first Castle, Collett unveiled the first King. Dismissed as a 'Super-Castle' by those envious of its overwhelming success, the outstanding feature of the new 4-6-0 express passenger engine was its unparalleled hauling power: a trac-

tive effort of 40,300 lbs psi — 27 per cent higher than Castle's. Boiler pressure was raised to 250 lbs psi using a new high pressure boiler, allied to a longer firebox with larger firegrate area and an increased total heating surface.

Kenneth Leech, living in Chippenham, was ideally placed in the heartland of 'King Country' to witness the daily performance of these engines designed particularly for the West of England expresses.

'I admired them for their sheer power and physical magnificence, and the steady feel of the footplate under one's feet. They'd run upto 90 mph, or more, on the level without any signs of distress or quivering through the frames.'

Kenneth's first-ever ride on a King was on the flagship engine No. 6000 *King George V*, affectionately known as 'The Bell' because of the brass bell mounted on her buffer beam, a momento of her highly acclaimed appearance in the United States at the centenary celebrations of the Baltimore

No.5351 on the Andover turn table sometime in 1956. The engine is lined green but had previously been painted all black. It had probably just worked a train from Cheltenham.

'I rode on this engine from Swindon to Andover and back. The old Midland and South Western Junction line ran through Swindon (High Level) from north to south over the Great Western, just west of Swindon main line station.

'This line continued running from north to south, and crossed the GW main line from Paddington to Westbury at Wolf Hall Savernake, and proceeded southwards to Andover (SR) where engines were turned for the northward return trip.'

No.5080 *Defiant* has enjoyed a chequered career. Built in May 1939, she originally entered service as *Ogmore Castle*, renamed *Defiant* in January 1941. After 1,117,030 miles service, she was withdrawn in April l963 and consigned to Barry scrapyard.

Fortunately, the engine was rescued by enthusiasts from the Birmingham Railway Museum, where she was later restored to full working order. The locomotive is now a prime attraction at Toddington on the Gloucestershire, Warwickshire Railway and is in demand for hauling enthusiasts' specials.

No.5547 just out of shops at Chippenham on 15 February 1958 with Driver Bill Bateman. 'On one auspicious occasion I rode on No 5547 with Bill Bateman at 70 mph through Box Station and round the curve!'

No.7030 *Cranbrook Castle*. 'I stood on the steps of Langley Crossing signal box to get this close-up of No.7030 on an up express. The double set of rails on the right are the down main line and the line of the dead-end goods siding, going right to clear the down main line.'

No.2937 *Clevedon Court* passes Chippenham West signal box on a down-train with Driver Clem Crook (Swindon) on the footplate.

& Ohio Railroad, in 1927.

'I found her a good engine, but no better than many others. She was sensitive to rail irregularities and from time to time at speed would suddenly come down hard with a bump and a crash'.

King's ran for more than two decades without major modification; but after the War and post-nationalisation, a series of important modifications were carried out in an endeavour to make them run faster, or pull heavier loads, or to make steam on poorer coal.

Following the sequential order in which each of the locomotive classes first made their appearance, we arrive at 1928 when the ubiquitous Halls first entered service; although the prototype No.2925 *Saint Martin*, rebuilt from a Churchward Saint, came out of shops in 1925. Previously, the semi-fast passenger and fast goods trains had been worked mainly by engines of the 43XX class, but the need for a more powerful engine for mixed traffic work had been evident for some time.

The success of the Halls can be judged by the number built (330) over a span of twenty-five years, and the fact they worked all over the Great Western system.

Kenneth Leech had a wide experience of Halls, riding on 187 different engines, a total of 550 trips. He drove on 239 occasions and fired 294 times.

Whilst the Hall, with driving wheels 6ft. diameter and a tractive effort of 27,275 lbs, was a great success, a need arose for a locomotive to deal with the heavier loads of fast goods and excursion trains. The answer was to be found in eighty engines of the Grange class, which replaced a number of less powerful and ageing 2-6-0s. A reduction in diameter of driving wheels by four inches from 6ft to 5ft 8ins put the tractive effort up to 28,875 lbs, an increase of 1,600 lbs over the Halls.

Kenneth's view is that on freights Granges just had the edge on Halls, on account of the smaller wheels and ability to move off from a standing start with comparative ease. 'I rode with them on expresses even though their first call was mixed traffic. Once I rode through Box Tunnel at 85 mph (10 mph over the speed restriction for the curve at Box). The engine was 6859 *Yiewsley Grange*. But Granges often did upto 90 with ease. Most exciting!'

Most of his runs on Granges were of short duration, even so, he clocked up 77 trips, driving on 37 and firing on 50. The apparent discrepancy in numbers is because sometimes he drove part way and fired the rest. 'In all I rode on fifty-two out of eighty engines. Some were the roughest I ever encountered; some the sweetest.'

The final 4-6-0 from the Collett stable was the Manor, a class designed and built to come within a definite weight limit and therefore it could not give the feeling of ample power as that of other 4-6-0s.

Kenneth rode on 11 of the 30 engines, always on stopping trains; he had no experience with Manors on expresses. The Counties were F W Hawksworth's only creation after he had succeeded C B Collett as Chief Mechanical Engineer of the Great Western. They were a post-war engine and preceded the BR standard locomotives. The new breed of engine had many detractors, for aesthetically they lacked the classical lines of their predecessors; there was something utilitarian about their appearance which reflected the dullness and austerity of the post-war period.

Kenneth rode on 22 out of 30 engines; a total of 143 trips. He drove 56 times and fired on 74 occasions. 'They were remarkable for sheer strength and rapid acceleration with a complete absence of slipping. 'I cannot recall a bad trip on a County. They were immensely strong, lively engines, but their riding always seemed to me to be a little harder than Castles.'

Swindon Works, October 1953. The shape of things to come. The lead engine in the line-up is No.2920 *Saint David*, the last Saint, just before scrapping. The old engine stood outside Swindon Works for upwards of a month while her future lay in the balance. Sadly, after a lifetime's sterling service, the decision to 'let her go' was taken. The second engine is No. 4056 *Princess Margaret* at works for her last general repair.

No.6812 *Chesford Grange* at Swindon Works sometime in 1957.

'Although none of my trips on Granges was of long duration, altogether I drove thirty-seven times and fired fifty times, riding on fifty-two out of the eighty engines of the Class. I agree with the view expressed by my friend, Driver Dick Potts, that on heavy freight trains Granges just had the edge on the Halls on account of their smaller wheels and ability to move off with comparative ease.'

Swindon Round House. A line-up of locomotives to set enthusiasts' hearts a flutter! The locomotives are:- No.4972 *Saint Bride's Hall* (far left), No.6832 *Brockton Grange*, No.6006 *King George I*, No.5091 *Cleeve Abbey*. Much of the foreground appears to be taken up by the shadow of the buffer the photographer was up against.

No.4960 *Pyle Hall* taking water on an up train at Creech Troughs. 'On one occasion, when No 6012 *King Edward VI* failed at Reading on the down *Riviera Limited*, No 4960 was the *Reading Pilot* and she took the train to Plymouth. She was shockingly rough, so that the inspector riding with us must have been scared, for he ordered the driver, an Old Oak Common friend of mine, not to exceed 70 mph. At first this limiting speed was adhered to, though not always!'

Chapter 6

Taking the Photographs

The first time Kenneth showed me some of his locomotive photographs (all neatly filed and precisely annotated) the thought nagged at the back of my mind: what sort of a camera had he used to take such superb photographs, many of them at train speed, and with such clarity?

Later, I peered through the viewfinder and clicked the shutter of a simple folding camera of German origin (manufacturer's name rubbed and illegible) which although, theoretically, second-hand had been bought new in Germany by a British soldier on demobilisation leave, and never used. It had an F3.5 lens and compur Rapid shutter, which Kenneth explained gave him a 1:400th sec. exposure, and which he 'helped' by panning the camera at half the estimated train speed.

Kenneth used mostly Ilford HP3 and HP4 film, and purchased ex-WD printing paper in quantities of 500 from a London supplier in 10' x 8' format for as little as £4.13.6d. (less than 1 pence per sheet in today's money) including carriage to Chippenham!

The exposed roll film was loaded into the developing tank, under Kenneth's bed-clothes, kneeling on the floor with his arms, head and shoulders covered and in darkness! Once in the developing tank, the actual developing, fixing and washing was, of course, a daylight job.

Kenneth's enlarger was certainly unique. It had started life as a horizontal gas-illuminated 'Magic Lantern' and needed appreciable modification to become an electrically-lit enlarger for small negatives, which it projected horizontally onto an engineer's drawing board, held upright by angle irons. The printing paper had to be fixed by pins at its four corners against the vertical face of the drawing board, so all genuine KHL enlargements are marked with four pin holes, one at each corner of the print!

Printing was undertaken by Kenneth in his wife's kitchen, with its wartime blackout curtains put over the windows; and at the height of his activities he was working five nights a week, frequently processing as many as twenty photographs a night.

Out of so many thousands was it possible to pick one particular shot as 'best photograph'? Such a trite question deserved Kenneth's sharp rejoiner:

'Of course not!' There were so many, each of them good for a particular reason. I can only say that I always took time and trouble before I pressed the shutter, and I felt at that moment I had used the best method possible.

'When photographing trains running at high speeds, for example, I always tried to capture the feeling of vivid action.'

Had he any regrets for missed opportunities; photographs he felt ought to have been taken?

'I'm sure there must have been quite a number, but I can't remember any. It's never been my wont to look back on my life with regret. But I do recall it was finding, after developing, that something I'd been

No.6876 *Kingsland Grange* picks up water from Creech Troughs. Date unknown, probably around 1954.

No.5082 *Swordfish*. 'This was my fourth photograph of a GWR engine and was probably taken in 1947 because No. 5082 still displays GWR livery. I took it at Langley Crossing, a mile east of Chippenham, on an up express. The down signal behind the train was soon to be re-located a lot further east − perhaps because the higher speeds of such trains as the *Bristolian* needed longer stopping distances.

'I had several excellent runs on No.5082. Once, on the Cambrian Coast Express, Driver Jermey put the engine up to just over 90 mph for my benefit. Yet on another trip, from Paddington, she would not steam, and had to be replaced by another engine at Swindon.'

No.6021 *King Richard II* heading the 10.35 am Paddington to Penzance express passing under the Somerset and Dorset Railway over-bridge at Cole on 6 August 1955. 'My friend and fellow enthusiast Patrick Garland was the observer on the far side of the line.'

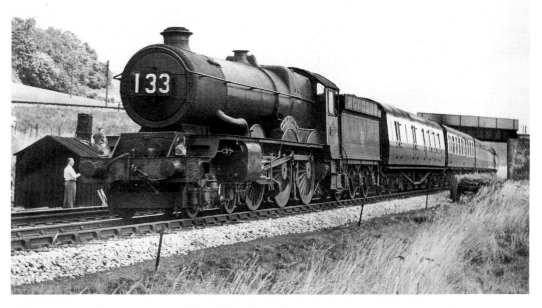

No.5076 *Gladiator*, about half a mile east of Chippenham station, with the 1.15 pm ex-Paddington express on 14 March 1953. First stop Bath.

No.7012 *Barry Castle*. 'I took this picture on 8 August 1954 just west of Swindon Station. The carriage works are in the background. It shows No.7012 on a South Wales train with a 15 x 8 load, and though steaming well, she took the banker through the Severn Tunnel.'

No.1021 *County of Montgomery* and No.4985 *Allesley Hall*. A high-speed pass at Whiteball on 7 August 1954.. No. 1021 on Paddington to Penzance and No. 4985 on 12.05 pm Paignton to Bristol. Both engines are in BR lined black livery, but otherwise in original condition.

doubtful about at the time had turned out satisfactorily that I wished I had persevered more.'

I put it to him, how might he have fared using an automatic single lens reflex camera, or even a modern day camcorder?

'I've never had the opportunity of trying a modern camera, and I can't say I'm impressed with all the paraphernalia. I've always believed in keeping things simple; and I must admit to having felt pleased with one or two of my more successful shots!'

He did admit, however, to having borrowed the Westinghouse Brake Company's movie camera on one auspicious occasion, back in 1938, to film the Great Northern Railway's Stirling 8-foot single, No.1, locomotive, brought out of retirement so that new Gresley stock could be given a demonstration run for journalists.

'To get the best results it was desirable to use most of the gadgets available, especially the long focus lens,·following the engine broadside at speeds up to nearly 70mph — but this was a unique cause and opportunity.'

Despite his frequent lineside visits Kenneth came to know only one other railway photographer of note, namely, R.C. 'Dick' Riley.

'I've always admired his work, not only for his skill and technique, but also for the great variety of his subject matter and the range of his photographic territory.'

A frequent visitor to engine sheds and locomotive works, it is perhaps surprising that Kenneth never met any of the official railway company photographers. However, several years ago I was instrumental, along with my friend, Driver Dick Potts, of Saltley, in introducing Kenneth to 90 year-old George Smith, who served as the Great Western's chief photographer, after being personally appointed by C.B.Collett.

We met at George's Swindon home where he and Kenneth swapped anecdotes and talked railways for many hours. But the strange thing was that George, unlike Kenneth, had not kept a single photograph from the thousands he had taken. From time to time, he had recognised several of his shots reproduced in books, and once had come across some of them framed and displayed in a public bar!

I asked Kenneth if he could remember the very last steam engine picture he had taken. 'I'm afraid not,' he replied, with conviction. 'I never look upon anything as being for the last time — it's far too painful!

So how would he liked to be remembered — as a railway photographer, or for his footplate experiences? Without a hint of hesitation came the surefire reply:

'Definitely, for my footplate experiences. Photography, by comparison, was but a passive interest.'

2-8-0 No.4700 at Chippenham on 31 July 1957 heading the 5.00 pm Swindon to Bristol train on a running-in turn.

'The 47XX class engines were renowned as supreme steam-raisers, but were awkward to fire because the distance from the coal pick-up on the tender to the firebox was about a foot less than on any other GW tender engines — and the firehole was higher!'

No.6001 *King Edward VII* on a test run at Hullavington on 2 July 1953. A speed of 60 mph was maintained up the bank with 26 coaches and 796 tons behind the tender. On this occasion No. 6001 was tested with an improvement to the single chimney and ran between Stoke Gifford and Scouts Lane, Reading.

No.5027 *Farleigh Castle* at Dauntsey Station, at the foot of the bank on 26 May 1961. 'I was on the footplate with Driver Tommy Worth ('He retired rather than drive diesels') and Chief Inspector Andress who had taken the regulator, for me to enjoy the speed of 90 mph.'

Acknowledgements

The authors wish to thank: Mr. Richard (Dick) Potts for advice in respect of locomotive mechanical detail, and in assisting with the selection of photographs. Mr. R.C. Riley for his helpful suggestions and reading the final manuscript. Mrs. Barbara Cleverley for typing the textmatter in its various and numerous stages.

Acknowledgement is also given to the following books as a valuable reference source:-

'Loco's of The Royal Road' – a new railway locomotive book for boys of all ages. W.G. Chapman (Great Western Railway. 1936).

'Famous Trains' – Cecil J. Allen (Meccano Library No.1. 1928).

'By Cornish Riviera Limited' – W.G. Chapman (George Routledge & Sons Ltd. 1936)

'Swindon Steam 1921-1951' – Kenneth J. Cook (Ian Allan. 1974).

Photograph:- Bryan Holden (left) and Kenneth Leech (right) with his model locomotive 'Emlyn' a GWR 4-2-2
Photograph by Chris Chard LMPA